NATIONAL GEOGRAPHIC

T0045068

Houses

Harley Chan

I live in a place that is very hot.

People here build houses
with clay.
Clay keeps houses cool inside.

I live in a place where it snows a lot.

People here build houses with strong, steep roofs.
The snow slides off the steep roofs.

I live in a place where it rains a lot.

People here build houses on stilts. Heavy rain can cause floods. Stilts keep the houses above the water.

I live in a place where
it is very rocky.
It is windy here, too.

People here build houses into the rocks.
The rocks protect the houses from the wind.